MAKING GOOD THINGS HAPPEN

The Atiku Abubakar Policy Document

Published by
Adonis & Abbey Publishers Ltd
P. O. Box 43418
London
SE11 4XZ
http://www.adonis-abbey.com
Email: editor@adonis-abbey.com

Second imprint: 2011

British Library Cataloguing-in-Publication Data
A catalogue record for this book is available from the
British Library

ISBN: 9781906704841

Layout Artist/Technical Editor, Jan B. Mwesigwa

Printed and bound in Great Britain

MAKING GOOD THINGS HAPPEN

The Atiku Abubakar Policy Document

by

Atiku Abubakar

Adonis & Abbey
Publishers Ltd

Table of Contents

SECTION I
EMPLOYMENT GENERATION
& WEALTH CREATION

SECTION II
INFRASTRUCTURE DEVELOPMENT

SECTION III
LAW & ORDER / CORRUPTION

SECTION IV
THE NIGER DELTA

SECTION V
EDUCATION & SOCIAL SERVICES

1. Economic Policy Working Group

1.1 Introduction

This document is the policy position of Atiku Abubakar. It is based on the premise that the Federal Government would be most effective by concentrating on a few priority areas. The critical areas include infrastructure development, job creation, security, the Niger Delta, good governance and war against corruption. The Federal Government can have significant and long-lasting impact on the lives of Nigerians by focusing on these five key areas. Further, the document sets out various initiatives for addressing issues associated with the five areas that will unleash the potentials inherent in the Nigerian economy.

Tackling the issues will require the cooperation of all stakeholders in the Nigerian Project, and the effective development of partnerships between various tiers of government, and between the government and the private sector. The initiatives are practical and achievable. Their attainment will require a paradigm shift change in the way the Federal Government operates, especially with a view to making it leaner, better managed and more result-oriented.

The urgent need for reform of the Nigerian economy and its sustenance is incontrovertible. The basic problems can be attributed to a mono-product economy with little domestic linkages characterised by the absence of basic services expected of a government and the inability of the system to enable individuals operate their lives and businesses with minimal interference by the government or its agencies. In recent years, the economic reform efforts have focussed on improving the macro-economy in the expectation that the benefits would subsequently accrue to those lower down the ladder. This is clearly not happening, with the resultant increase in income inequalities, joblessness and general insecurity. It is, therefore, important that the current reform efforts are given added impetus, and that the benefits are better targeted. Without this, the public support necessary for the success of the reforms will not be sustained.

Central to the future reform efforts is a re-view, and revision, of the role of the state. There is need to revisit the role of the Nigerian state in development with a view to assuming a more active role in promoting market based mechanisms albeit with the state as an enabler for the private sector. Given Nigeria's growth ambitions and the need to accelerate economic growth and development, the state must take an active role in ensuring accelerated infrastructure development. A laissez faire approach that relies solely on market efficacy cannot deliver the results expected to be achieved within the next decade.

The initiatives outlined have the following themes:

- Identification of and focus on mission critical areas
- Emphasis on sectors with significant multiplier effects on the rest of the economy e.g., infrastructure; agriculture; human capital development

This document provides the framework for the implementation of the policies of Atiku Abubakar. Its implementation will require a nexus of partnerships between the Federal, State and Local governments (3G partnership) and the Public Private Sector Partnership (PPP) particularly because; a) areas such as education, agriculture and health are best delivered at the state level, and b) given the limitations in the Federal government's resources, private sector funding is required if a greater quantum of funds is to be mobilised for developmental purposes.

1.2 Background

Nigeria is today at crossroads. The Olusegun Obasanjo administration witnessed a modest turnaround in Nigeria's economy, including the introduction of some initiatives that have the potential of accelerating Nigeria's economic growth. Amongst others, the factors responsible for the turnaround to date and greater optimism include:

- The pension fund reforms
- The global commodity boom leading to sustained increase in oil prices
- Better fiscal management
- Stable exchange rate underpinned by increased foreign exchange reserves
- Paris club debt relief
- Institutionalisation of due process procurement mechanism
- Privatisation/liberalisation thereby creating greater opportunities for the local business class
- Increased non-oil foreign direct investment (especially in telecoms and banking etc) and increased foreign portfolio investment
- Improved agricultural production and productivity

The benefits of growth, however, are generally perceived to be primarily limited to the upper strata of the society. While the changes have resulted in positive GDP growth, a lot remains to be done to ensure sustained accelerated economic growth that directly affect the middle-class and the poor particularly in areas such as health services, quality education, food, clothing and affordable housing. Amongst the factors militating against a broader economic recovery with greater linkages and impact on employment and poverty are:

- Inadequate and decaying infrastructure
- Weak real sector
- Insecurity and the increasing inability of the state to impose its authority over certain sectors of the economy and parts of the country
- Low purchasing power
- Rising income inequalities/Failure of the expected economic trickle down, which could stall the reform momentum
- Insufficient linkages between the growth sectors and the rest of the economy.
- Continued rent seeking activities (especially in the petroleum sector)

Rising income inequalities coupled with concentration of the benefits of economic growth within a tiny minority have led to reduced support for the economic reform efforts of the government. To sustain public acceptability for the reform programme, the benefits must be felt by the totality of Nigerians. It is, therefore, critical that the next government makes a determined effort to build upon the successes recorded in recent years and ensure that the "dividends of democracy" are enjoyed by the totality of Nigerians.

The challenge is achieving sustainable economic growth that translates into real change in the lives of the vast majority of Nigerians. In doing so, a coherent set of policies is required.

The five (5) priorities are:

1. Employment generation and wealth creation
2. Power generation and infrastructure development
3. Education and social services
4. Law & order, good governance and war against corruption
5. The Niger Delta

It is intended that this policy document shall provide the conceptual framework for the development of an Atiku Abubakar administration, which should lead to Nigeria's transformation into a modern economy. The policy framework from development to implementation to general benefits would on average take some time to be fully realised. However, notwithstanding, there must be some immediately discernible and tangible benefits to Nigerians within the first twelve (12) months of an Atiku

Abubakar administration. The approach adopted is, therefore, to identify quick wins achievable within the first twelve (12) months, and thereafter, medium term initiatives realisable during the four-year life of the government. They have therefore been presented in that order.

1. To identify the problems associated with each of the above areas (<u>The</u> issues).
2. To define ways, means and timelines for solving these problems (<u>The Initiatives</u>).
3. Determine sources of and methods for funding the solutions (<u>cost</u>).

The initiatives that follow are proposed to be implemented within three timelines namely:

*   First hundred (100) days of the administration,
*   Short term i.e. within twelve (12) months of the commencement of the new administration; and
*   The medium term i.e., within four (4) years.

SECTION I

EMPLOYMENT GENERATION
& WEALTH CREATION

2. Job Creation

2.1 Job Creation

2.1 (a) The Issues

From surveys conducted nationwide, the single most important issue for most Nigerians today is job creation. In spite of the economic growth recorded in recent years, the economy is simply not growing quickly enough to absorb the numbers joining the labour market each year. Furthermore, economic growth recorded in the last five (5) years has had little effect in creating sustainable jobs, thereby leading to a reduction of public support for much needed economic reforms. The problem is made more acute by the fact that a significant number of seemingly employed individuals are under-employed and, therefore, not operating to their maximum potential.

Previous government job creation efforts have proceeded by actively seeking to create specific categories of jobs for the unemployed. In recent years, government has realised the futility of this approach, and instead, efforts are now being placed on providing a conducive environment for the creation of jobs. That should be government's primary role in job creation initiatives.

Government must, directly or through PPPs and/or the 3G partnership, play an active role in providing an enabling environment for:

1. The development of entrepreneurs through high impact job creation initiatives, who will in turn employ others,
2. Encouraging infrastructure development that is inherently labour intensive (especially in conjunction with the private sector);
3. Resuscitation of industrial activity as a fall out of the improved infrastructure e.g. power
4. Accelerating the growth/opening up other service sectors that are labour intensive

    a. Law and order
    b. Teaching
    c. Health services
    d. Sports and entertainment

2.1 (b) The Initiatives

2.1 (b) (i) High Impact job creation

In considering job creation, government should aim to limit the entry into lost causes (i.e., those without skills and who do not have any incentive to seek jobs because there are alternative and more beneficial paybacks). High impact job creation is to be anchored on encouraging entrepreneurs as well as job opportunities through national priority projects in labour intensive infrastructure development (road and rail track development; development of a gas pipeline network; affordable housing etc).

1st 90 days

- Set up a manpower agency to act as a job agency where jobseekers meet job providers.
- Streamline the activities of the various job creation agencies to ensue objectives are harmonised and efforts are better channelled to reflect government's priorities;

Short Term

- Provide incentives to the jobless by changing the incentive structure

    - increasing salaries of teachers and health workers,
    - Provide vocational/skills acquisition training to a minimum of 200,000 potential entrepreneurs

- Assisting the growth of the entertainment industry expecially Nollywood by

    - Ensuring access to bank financing

- Reviewing the existing copyright laws to protect budding Nigerian artistes and culture

Medium-Term (within 4 years)

- Develop skilled workers who will add value to the economy. These workers shall be empowered:

  - Provide vocational training and skill acquisition programmes to 1,000,000 people to enable potential entrepreneurs acquire accounting, management training expertise etc;
  - Strengthen SMEDAN (both capacity and quality) to:

    - provide business support/advisory services etc
    - champion policies for SME growth;

  - Actively provide support to and work with non-governmental organisations with similar objectives.

- Develop/enhance existing skill centres to support the areas the government is emphasising (construction; teaching; health workers, information, communications and technology).

- Facilitate development of private sector micro-credit structures/windows to support aspiring businesspeople:

  - complement business advisory support work of SMEDAN and other relevant NGOs
  - Provide entrepreneurs with better access to credit by attracting a minimum of $250 million of private sector funding (excluding SMIEIS) for Nigerian small businesses

- Develop sports and sporting facilities (gyms, leisure centres) under a 3G partnership as well as via PPPs

  - Sports and leisure activities have been neglected despite the fact that they offer job opportunities and significant social mobility potential;
  - Establish a network of community and leisure centres in at least every local government area in the country.

- Actively promote Nollywood to make it the 3rd largest film industry in the world by:

  - encouraging partnerships between banks and Nollywood to deepen access to bank funding,

- assisting via the Nigerian Film Corporation and private sector initiatives, enhancements in film production capabilities and technology,
- An initiative to access new markets in Africa, the diaspora, the Black world, and Asia;
- improved distribution networks nationwide and outside Nigeria, and generally facilitate their integration into the formal economy
- Passage of a revised copyrights Act
- Strict enforcement of the copyright laws

- The largest creator of jobs worldwide is law and order. Jobs in the law and order sector to be developed by:

  - Outsourcing basic security services in government offices
  - Encouraging private sector security firms to expand their scope to effectively complement the Police.

- Utilise agriculture as a means for creating both rural and urban jobs

  - As a social responsibility. While this may not meet a conventional cost benefit test, it will open up opportunities and provide the fulcrum to enable people farm even on a subsistence basis.

- These efforts shall be complemented with provision of micro credit;
- Better access to inputs and farm extension services; and
- Reorganisation, strengthening and re-capitalisation of the Nigerian Agriculture, Cooperative and Rural Development Bank to facilitate loans to smaller farmers.

- Create linkages between infrastructure development and job creation

    - Specific initiatives will include using as much local input as possible in developing new rail tracks (i.e., integrating Ajaokuta and Delta Steel into the new infrastructure programme)

These shall be primarily private sector initiatives but with government acting as an enabler.

2.2 Economic Transformation

Job creation must be complemented with economic transformation. Economic transformation in this context refers to changes with the capacity to have a deep and meaningful impact on the Nigerian economy. Some of the economic transformation initiatives are outlined within the Infrastructure section (steady electricity supply and development of a modern road and rail network, development of a gas pipeline network). Others include restructuring the Federal Government and implementation of property reforms.

In achieving transformation, attention needs to be paid to comparative advantage. In certain circumstances, comparative advantage can be created, and we need not therefore assume it a natural endowment. The concept of comparative advantage should be linked with SMEs in order to develop value adding products/activities where Nigeria can develop a comparative advantage over a period. Government can create the enabling environment for this to be achieved.

2.2 (a) Land Ownership and Property Rights Reform

The big enabler of any people is the land tenure system. In a functional market economy such as we aspire to have, individuals must have clearly-defined and inalienable property rights. The absence of effective property rights is partly responsible for the inability of large numbers of Nigerians to take advantage of the economic reform and formal credit/banking system. Macroeconomic policies can liberalise sectors and open up opportunities but unless economic agents are able to mobilise and take advantage of the opportunities, they will not feel the impact of the reforms.

Many Nigerians own land that is untitled, and therefore of no use whatsoever in facilitating access to capital or freeing up tied capital. Instead, land is typically held through informal arrangements that have local relevance but cannot be used in the formal economy. Macroeconomic reforms, desirable as they are, cannot achieve their intended objectives unless a serious and concerted effort is made to vest formal title in landowners. Formal title will integrate the poor and the marginalised into the formal economy and enable them leverage their assets to further their well-being by seeking to achieve their individual or community pursuits.

Nigeria therefore needs to make an outright commitment to title all land. This will immediately transform a fixed and illiquid asset into a valuable asset capable of generating capital for investment with consequent wealth creation.

Allied to the property reforms are availability of affordable housing and mortgage reforms. Nigeria faces a severe housing deficit. Estimates by the Federal Mortgage Bank indicate a deficit of at least 12 million housing units. While the deficit cannot be addressed within the lifetime of an administration, a concerted effort at reducing is however clearly required. This will entail creating linkages between provision of land to property developers, increased availability of housing finance, reduction in property transaction costs and job creation across several sectors ancillary to provision of additional housing stock.

Macroeconomic stability is critical in mobilising housing finance (as a result of its impact in ensuring a low rate of inflation, affordable interest rates and in increasing household and corporate savings). The pension reforms will provide a long term funding market, which subject to macro economic stability will facilitate the development of the mortgage market. Coherent action is therefore required to increase home ownership and broaden the potential outlets for pension fund assets.

2.2 (a) (i) The Initiatives

Short-Term

- Government shall encourage home ownership and give added impetus to home ownership by introducing tax incentives via mortgage interest relief whereby homebuyers can offset a proportion of their mortgage interest payments against their tax liability.

- Encourage a review of pension fund investment guidelines to facilitate enhanced pension fund involvement in provision of financing necessary for the development of the Nigerian mortgage market.
- Enact appropriate foreclosure and securitisation legislation to mobilise additional housing finance.
- Reduce property transaction costs (stamp duties and other charges).

Medium Term

- Facilitate an increase in housing stock via 3G and PPP partnerships as well as through housing finance reforms.
- Under a 3G partnership (since land matters are a residual responsibility), title, record and map all landed assets in the country. The Federal Government shall achieve this by introducing an initiative that has nationwide acceptance thereby encouraging the States to follow suit.
- Review of the Land Use Act and the passage of a revised Land Use Act that is more market friendly while protecting the rights of small holders and the landless
- Recapitalise the Federal Mortgage Bank through a partial privatisation in order to allow it play an expanded role in the secondary mortgage market

2.3 Petrochemicals

2.3 (a) *The Issues*

- Need to find a way to add value to the local economy via strategic linkages. Development of a petrochemicals industry will allow the country to impact upon so many sectors –

  - agriculture (85% urea based);
  - pharmaceuticals (almost wholly reliant on imported raw materials);
  - textiles;
  - food technology;
  - fishing vessels;
  - construction/building materials;
  - fibres;
  - polyesters;
  - soaps
  - Tyres

- Creation of petrochemical jobs will be significantly accelerated by generating processed local raw materials, especially for SMEs. UNIDO estimates of up to 1 million new jobs can be created in Nigeria within 10 years via petrochemicals/petrochemicals based activities.

- Capacity exists in Warri; Kaduna; Eleme and Port Harcourt.

2.3 (b) The Initiatives

Medium-Term

- Support will be given to companies operating in the petrochemicals industry

  - pioneer industry status;
  - preferential gas availability and
  - attractive pricing to enable them operate at full capacity.

3. Macroeconomic Framework

3.1 The Issues

In recent years, Nigeria has performed relatively well on the macroeconomic front. The performance has been anchored largely on the global commodity price booms rather than structural changes in the economy. In the last three (3) years, all major emerging market countries have amassed strong reserves largely due to the global commodity boom. Commodity prices have been driven higher by strong growth in China and major industrial economies. Within that context, Nigeria's reserves are below emerging market averages.

GDP growth has been fuelled largely by services and agriculture. Nigeria has recorded up to six (6) percent per annum GDP growth, but with more effective policies, this could be ramped up to about 10% per annum. Crop production, retail trade and telecoms have been the highest growth contributors to the economy, while sectors such as cement, water transport, rail transport and pipelines have provided growth challenges. While economic growth has undoubtedly been recorded and has offered new opportunities for new investments, the Nigerian economy has generally underperformed.

Government has been unable to use fiscal policy to stimulate the economy. Overall, capital expenditure as a percentage of GDP has been declining while recurrent expenditure has been on the upward trend i.e., the cost of running government is increasing – hence the increase in recurrent expenditure that is clearly not sustainable. Fiscal policy is not being effectively used to accelerate the growth rate – in nominal terms, the economy has been growing faster than the budget, implying that the economy does have the absorptive capacity to absorb some of the excess earnings from crude oil exports

Fiscal policy is, therefore, having limited impact on the economy, which necessitates a fundamental reassessment of the budgeting process

3.1 (a) The Initiatives

3.1 (a) (i) Inflation

Short-Term

- The Federal Government will define a clear-cut policy target for the life of the administration

- Cause the CBN to create a semi-autonomous banking supervision function within the CBN, thereby allowing CBN to concentrate on its key mandate of pursuing price stability and focusing on monetary policy

Medium-Term

- Pursue a sustained low inflation policy in order to achieve stable and low interest rates
- Focus the Central Bank on its key price stability mandate by specifying clear inflation targets, which CBN will be required to deliver.
- Provide the CBN with **operational independence in accordance with its charter**, while the strategic independence should reside with the political leadership.

    - If the targets are missed, CBN should be sanctioned accordingly. CBN will thus become an instrument for delivering the results.
    - Review the CBN charter and consider the workability of a banking supervision agency working independently of, but in collaboration with the CBN

3.1 (a) (ii) Reserve Management:

Short-Term

- Introduce in-house reserve management of a proportion of the foreign reserves within CBN by hiring some of the best asset management professionals globally who will operate within the CBN based on globally acceptable asset management standards;
- Accelerate local reserve management albeit with the concept of "readiness" i.e., factor in the skills shortages and accelerate skill acquisition.
- Actively encourage global reserve management players interested in Nigeria's reserves to set up operations in Nigeria;
- Reassess the holdings of the nations reserves in US Dollars (gold, an alternative, has appreciated 60% in the last year) and establish an optimal asset mix which shall be reviewed on a regular basis.

3.1 (a) (iii) Budgeting process

1st 90 days

- Create a dedicated Office of Management & Budget within the Presidency, which will be charged with a developmental focus in budgeting.

Short-term

- Quantify budgetary leakages and redirect to priority savings to priority areas (education, health, funding of revised compensation structure). Based on the above, deliverables can be specified and monitored accordingly.
- Improve the budgeting process to facilitate more effective budget impact on the economy by undertaking quarterly appraisals and communicating the status.
- Provide explicit commitments/promises, which translate into specific deliverables.
- Specify expenditure targets for priority sectors (e.g. education and health) as a percentage of GDP, and undertake specific initiatives to achieve the targets.
- Separate the office of the Accountant – General of the Federation (who shall be responsible for the Federation Accountant) from that of the Accountant General of the Federal Government (who will have responsibility for Federal Government's finances).
- Overhaul and institutionalise the due process mechanism to enable accelerated public procurement without compromising quality or costs.
- Ensure better planning across government by including all agencies within the 3-year medium term expenditure reviews, and

making the outcome publicly available information.

Medium-Term

- Ensure government wide adherence to the 3-year medium term expenditure framework.
- Improve quality of government expenditure by complementing the work of the due process office with operational independence for the office of the Auditor-General of the Federation, who shall be required to present his report within 6 months of the end of each budget year.
- Ensure better planning by government agencies thereby preventing bottlenecks being created due to bunching of project approval requests at the due process office.
-
- Ensure streamlined due process system/fast track procurement process:

    - review the budgeting process and create additional capacity in federal agencies/ departments etc,
    - reside due process functions in the ministries under sector specialists rather than a central due process office;
    - develop a better procurement process so that early planning is factored in; and

- ensure only projects with due process pre-certification are included in the budget.

4. The Presidency – Operating Arrangments

Medium-Term

The initiatives for improving the efficiency of the office of the President include:

- A strong commitment to Federalism as the basis for cooperation amongst all tiers of government

    - The Presidency shall use the Office of President to achieve the objectives of Federalism, and thereby expand the scope so that exclusive powers are not used as exclusive operating powers;
    - Create a structure/mechanism for transferring additional powers to states with FGN providing/defining standards (e.g., Education; Agriculture; Health)

- Create a mechanism through which the Presidency can obtain feedback from the public. There must be regular interaction between the leader and the people
- A concerted effort to do away with micromanagement of issues by the Presidency. This requires a very high quality of public appointees – indeed, one of the most important factors is the quality of

important factors is the quality of cabinet appointees and the senior civil service.

- A systemic change is required to be put in place
- The President shall assemble an effective team and empower them so that he remains a macro player.
- Government will actively engage the best no matter the constraints, empower them, delegate responsibility and create a policy monitoring mechanism for assessing performance of appointees.
- Review the size of government – merge functions presently undertaken by some ministries and agencies so that a smaller, leaner government is created

- Government's processes/systems must be streamlined so that businesses are not constrained by bureaucracy.

  - Presently, there is disconnect between the various departments in government (that is, government becomes an obstacle due to turf battles) and this has adverse consequences on general development.

- An annual State of the Economy speech shall be given by the President outlining the key issues and implications.

SECTION II

INFRASTRUCTURE
DEVELOPMENT

5. Power Sector

5.1 The Issues

The absence of a stable and effective power system is perhaps the single most important factor militating against a sustained growth of the Nigerian economy. Governments have in the past made promises on improvements in electricity supplies all of which have failed to materialize. It is estimated that a stable electricity supply system will lead to a 25 percent increase in the rate of economic growth.

The power sector is presently in a crisis, and the Nigerian people expect the next government to ensure that the electricity supply situation records a significant year on year improvement within the shortest possible time. Indeed the success or otherwise of the next government may be determined largely by whether or not it is able to improve the power supply crisis.

The national grid presently operates on a radial system, which is extremely fragile and prone to breakdowns. Due to the fragility of the national grid, generation levels above 3,500MW frequently lead to national system collapses. Construction of new power stations, rehabilitation and expansion of transmission and distribution networks are currently underway to bridge the electricity supply gap. These include the eleven host power plants being constructed by government, which are expected to be commissioned by the end of May 2007.

Seven of the plants are in the Niger Delta, and are being developed under the aegis of the National Integrated Power Project (NIPP). The other four include three that are being constructed using "soft loans" provided by the Chinese government – in Ajaokuta, Geregu and Papalanto. There are also other private independent power projects, some of which have come on stream or under construction, for example, AGIP and SHELL plants, respectively. Altogether, the government is committed to generating at least 10,000 MW by the end of 2007.

Given the realities prevalent in the electricity sector, namely, inefficient operational and financial performance, inadequate transmission and distribution infrastructure, poor payment and collection culture and dearth of investment capital, supplying the electricity produced to consumers and collecting concomitant revenues may provide serious challenges in the short-term. In addressing the inadequate supply infrastructure, government is closing the gap in the transmission network thereby making it a proper grid system as opposed to a radial system. This will make the system more reliable and less prone to national system collapses. Although distribution is receiving attention, it is, however, not certain that a clear policy on how to bridge the infrastructure gap at this level is being adequately addressed.

Ostensibly, there are some critical issues that have to be addressed if generation, transmission and distribution are to improve substantially to improve the quantity and quality of electricity services to the generality of Nigerians. These include:

5.1 (a) Institutional and Structural Arrangement

I. Continued restructuring of institutional and organizational structure of the industry premised on competition and choice

II. Clear definition on the role of government to focus on policy formulation, direction for the industry, support and legislation, while the role of the private sector will focus on operation and development of the industry

III. Independent and effective economic and technical regulation to attract private sector participation and investment while concomitantly protecting the public interest

IV. Appropriate industry structure will have to be based on the overarching objective of providing electricity services to the generality of Nigerians at reasonable costs while ensuring the financial viability and long-term development of the industry

5.1 (b) Infrastructure

I. Although government set a target of 10,000MW and is currently developing eleven power stations to realize this target, it is doubtful if 10,000MW will meet the medium-term electricity requirement of the country talkless of energy required to meet the goals and objectives of NEEDS and MDGs.

II. Although transmission network is being reinforced and expanded to make it more reliable and less susceptible to national outages, the on-going transmission plan is hinged on 10,000MW. As stated in 2(a) significant investment in transmission infrastructure will be required if the quality of service is to improve particularly as the preponderance of power plants are being constructed in the southern part of the country.

III. The distribution sector is the weakest link in the electricity chain. The estimated technical distribution losses, non-technical losses and collection losses are approximately seven (7), twenty seven (27), and twenty three (23) percent, respectively. The implication is that more than half of electricity generated, from a revenue collection perspective, is not accounted for.

IV. Inadequate metering, as captured in non-technical losses, is an issue that is capable of seriously undermining the viability and long-term development of the industry. To address this problem, a far-reaching and widespread metering programme will have to be embarked upon to ensure that all consumers of electricity pay for what they rightfully consume.

5.1 (c) Operational

I. It is important that fuel availability, particularly gas supply, is improved upon to reduce the adverse impact of interruptions in gas supply that have become manifest with Niger Delta strife and maintenance of Nigerian Gas Company pipelines.

II. Development of gas supply infrastructure outside the Niger Delta area (to other parts of the country not currently served) to allow the siting of power plants closer to load (consumption) centres. Since modern power plants have capacities to use dual fuel, the disruption caused by pipeline vandalisation will be isolated and mitigated.

III. In the long term, electricity generation plant mix will need to be diversified to include non-renewable energy (hydro, solar, nuclear) and other thermal fuels (coal, bio-fuel) thereby reduce dependence on natural gas in light of the strife in the Niger Delta while concomitantly improving security of supply.

IV. Currently, pricing and electricity tariffs are inadequate to cover cost of providing electricity services. To encourage investment and ensure viability of the industry, prices must perforce be cost reflective. This responsibility falls under the purview of the Nigerian Electricity Regulatory Commission (NERC).

V. Other issues that are capable of undermining the financial and operational performance of the industry are the legacy and other debts[1] (including pension liabilities). It is imperative that these are addressed. The two policy options are government assuming the bulk of the debts and defray with budgetary provisions or the debts left within the industry and dealt with by increasing end-user tariffs.

VI. With the best of intention and purpose vis-à-vis efficient provision of services, revenue shortfall will persist in light of the quantum

---

[1] The recent Paris club Debt relief will positively affect the debt stock of the industry.

of losses prevalent in the industry. Similar to (e) above, the two options are government to provide support and/or allow prices to increase to a level high enough to cover the shortfalls.

VII. To encourage private investment, government will have to institute a set of fiscal and investment incentives.

5.2 The Initiatives

Nigeria is committed to achieving the Millennium Development Goals. To halve poverty by 2015, the Nigerian economy must grow at an annual rate of seven (7) percent. There is a high correlation between GDP growth and availability of electricity (a factor of 1.25). That is,, for every 1% GDP growth, a 1.25% growth in power supply is required. Based on some preliminary assessment, by 2011 Nigeria will need 13,000 MW of available generation capacity, and 20,000MW by 2015.

A National priority programme will therefore be required to provide an additional minimum of 1000MW pa between 2007 and 2012 to reach 15,000MW. Developing new stations is a medium term approach because it will take at least two and a half years to construct a conventional power station.

Short-Term

Adopt a 2 tiered approach – an emergency power programme **(EPPs)** that can deliver additional capacity in certain key areas (as was done with AES in Lagos and Geometeric & Aggrecko in Abuja), and also ensure the completion of the power plants, distribution and transmission infrastructure currently under construction, and a National Power Programme (NPP) to be pursued over the medium-term.

EPPs will be undertaken as a short-term measure to ensure enhanced supply within the first year of the new administration:

- Provide EPPs for key urban areas (Lagos, Port Harcourt, Abuja, Kaduna, Onitsha; Kano) but taking into account the need to provide investors with a reasonable return in the pricing decisions;
- Ensure an accelerated procurement cycle to achieve timely delivery of the EPPs
- Consider acquiring excess capacity from Eastern Europe/other such areas, although care will be taken to ensure a transparent procurement process
- Undertake tariff adjustments to make it viable for operators/ government to make the new investment in the industry.
- Commercial rates to be charged in commercial areas. (this may also be used as a

mechanism to allow cities to reclaim their commercial areas).

Medium-Term

Under the NPP, pursue a 2 pronged approach

1. Complete ongoing system expansion to increase supply; and
2. Undertake a holistic reform (restructuring and private sector participation).

   a. Implement an integrated approach; as allied industries – gas development must be linked to power.
   b. Achieve an efficient use of resources and demand side management (development and commitment to a long term industry development plan);
   c. Efficient load management with priority given to wealth creating activities
   d. Development of alternative energy sources - Nuclear power for the long term (i.e., upon exhaustion of gas although the needed research and development work should commence within the life of the next administration)

e. FGN to encourage private sector in generation and distribution, and provide incentive schemes;

f. Ensure adequate power off-take arrangements including where appropriate, direct support from government.

g. Improve the transmission network so that a closed circuit exists to replace the present radial network

h. Privatisation to be pursued alongside restructuring. The sector restructuring will be fast tracked while simultaneously pursuing privatisation.

i. Liberalisation will continue apace with efforts being taken at the Local and State Government level too as power is on the concurrent list.

j. Consultation: All strata must be made aware of the developmental role of power and the need to incorporate it into the reform efforts. All stakeholders shall be carried along (States; Local Governments etc).

k. FGN will in consultation with other stakeholders, utilize some excess crude earnings to provide additional generation and distribution capacity.

l. Assess the configuration of distribution sector.

6. Micro Initiatives

Private sector to be encouraged to provide power to certain areas based on mini generation schemes in return for a services charge;

- Reduce generators operating within an area and encourage the development of "mega" generators in neighbourhoods.
- Shall be on an incentive-based structure rather than via coercion.
- FGN to provide support for cities and states to develop framework required for facilitating cooperation between individuals; Operators can secure sites and provide power for particular areas

6.1 Gas

- Undertake a review of and develop a new gas fiscal regime. Gas fiscal regime presently provides little incentive for the deep development of the gas sector. It must be reviewed to encourage reduced flaring and greater utilisation in power generation.
- Develop gas supply infrastructure while minimising flaring especially developing the gas pipeline along Oben- Abuja – Kaduna – Kano as a priority project.

6.1 (a) Power Sector Institutional Mechanism

1st 100 days

- Appoint a fully empowered individual with sufficient authority across all the relevant sectors/government agencies to spearhead the power reforms ("power sector czar").
- All government agencies MUST cooperate on the priority projects. Presently, liaison between agencies (customs; immigration, ports, FIRS) is very weak and bedeviled by conflict.
- It MUST be made very clear to government agencies that all the reforms /changes are predicated upon government speaking with one voice.

Short-term

- Strengthen regulation (a better equipped and positioned NERC and make more effective. Based on the close interplay between gas and electricity, close co-ordination between the two sectors (and regulation) is imperative;
- Review the role of the Ministry of Petroleum Resources; restructure into a Ministry of Energy covering power and gas;
- Abolish Ministry of Steel and transfer its functions to Ministry of Industries

- Set targets and develop appropriate model for increasing rural access

6.2 Transportation

6.3 The Issues

- The Nigerian transport system is primarily unimodal – over 90% of freight and passengers move by road. The system lacks intermodal connectors
- Unimodalism has been encouraged by a lack of regulation (lack of axle load controls and low market entry barriers favour road transport and further distort the market). The net result is a system with low efficiency, and high transport and maintenance costs;
- Lack of intermodal coordination has led to

    - (a) fragmented planning as e.g. exemplified by the non-prioritisation of the Jebba - Kaduna road despite the fact that it is critical from a road user's perspective,
    - (b) sub-optimal resource allocation e.g., the Inland Container Depot (ICD) project has not prioritised the need to decongest Lagos, and

- (c) port concessioning without factoring in the efforts to revitalise rail and hinterland connections;

- Road transport will still remain the principal transport mode for the foreseeable future, and therefore requires attention while creating a level playing field with other forms of transport;

- Lagos, with its limited transport infrastructure, is the primary gateway for foreign trade and therefore dominates national transportation activity thus resulting in significant transport congestion; The bulk of the transport distortions start and have their resolution in Lagos;

- Limited rail connectivity forces goods onto road transport (up to 300 trucks are needed daily to carry containers through the Lagos metropolitan area; very slow transit times – 5 – 25km per hour through Lagos; Long port stays – 8 to 11 days compared to 2 day averages elsewhere in West Africa;

- Additional sea freight congestion charges due to delays in Lagos could add N29.9 billion ($230 million) per annum to transport costs in 2006 alone;

- Agricultural products are dominant in some parts of the country (Middle Belt; Northern Cross River state, between Jos Plateau and

Benue River; Kaduna/Kano axis), and commodity movement from surplus to demand areas (urban areas in South and Central Nigeria) is very significant for transport flows. Efficient linkages between agricultural production and consumption zones are therefore urgently required;

- Bulk of the transport activity is along three corridors, and traffic volumes are expected to double within the next 20 years:

  - Lagos to Kano (Western Corridor)
  - Port Harcourt to Kaduna (Eastern corridor)
  - Lagos to Cross River (West – East Corridor)

- Fragmentation in policy making and regulatory responsibilities with four different ministries involved in aspects of transportation (Ministries of Transport; Aviation; Works; and Agriculture and Rural Development), and policy confusion and jurisdictional overlap between the ministries and their respective agencies.

Resolution of the transportation problems requires undertaking a combination of general and specific initiatives.

6.4 The Initiatives

6.4 (a) *General Initiatives*

Short-Term

- Introduce a new national transport regulation system to ensure balanced regulation and that users pay close to the real cost of road use
- Develop a new National Transport Policy that addresses issues relevant to promote intermodalism including institutional fragmentation, intermodal regulation, intermodal connectors and measuring transport system performance.
- Involve all stakeholders in developing the new policy especially state and Local Governments in respect of roads and passenger traffic, and operators, service providers and users with respect to barriers to efficiency
- Achieve policy consistency and effective regulatory framework by vesting the Ministry of Transport with policy and regulatory oversight.
- Develop Public Private Sector Partnerships (PPP) for the development of the transport infrastructure.

Medium-Term

- Enhance linkages to agricultural zones and develop agricultural collection and distribution hubs (Jebba Lafia; Makurdi; Lokoja; Pategi/Baro; Shendam; Jalingo)

    - Develop/rehabilitate the connecting road networks under a 3G partnership
    - Provide incentives to the private sector to establish commercially viable collection facilities
    - Provide federal support for development of infrastructure for the distribution hubs

- Encourage clustering of industrial activities in zones around Enugu, Oshogbo, Onne, Benin, Suleija, Zaria, Calabar, Maiduguri, Gombe, Sokoto, Gusau and Jos

    - Create industrial zones under PPPs, and concession them out to private operators
    - FGN to assist the private sector by funding 50% of the cost of the primary infrastructure in the industrial zones
    - FGN shall ensure availability of power in the industrial zones

- Develop inland dry ports

- Define timelines for completion of con-
cessions granted from inland/dry port
development

- Emphasise intermodalism – characterised by
coordinated planning and building of transport infrastructure; seamless operations
(road/rail/air/road); efficient infrastructural
and operational linkages; and modal choice
- New road developments to feed into the
economic activity points, from which states
can develop trunk roads to feed into the
new national network. The critical links to
be (re)developed include

  - Lagos – Ibadan
  - Lagos – Abuja
  - Lagos – Benin City via Ijebu-Ode
  - Asaba - Onitsha
  - Owerri – Port Harcourt
  - Jebba – Tegina – Kaduna
  - Abuja – Jos – Maiduguri
  - Abuja - Makurdi

- Improve Lagos port efficiency and achieve
accelerated development of Onne Port as an
alternative container port
- Connect ports to the national road and rail
network in particular, redevelop rail links to
Apapa, Tin Can and Onne
- Undertake lasting reconstruction of roads

- Establish regular rail freight operations and induce a modal shift from road to rail

6.4 (b) Specific Initiatives

6.4 (b) (i) Railways

Short-Term

- Conduct a detailed feasibility study to determine whether to expand the network using the standard gauge or to remain with the narrow gauge system.

Medium-Term

- Nigeria uses narrow gauge tracks that can be used into the foreseeable future primarily for freight at an estimated maintenance cost of $60-80m per annum;
- The standard gauge system exists around the Ajaokuta- Warri- Itakpe axis. This will be extended to Abuja so that Warri shall over the long term become the port servicing Abuja.
- Develop the Lagos – Abuja rail network on the standard gauge system
- Undertake a programme of rehabilitating/upgrading the existing rail network.
- Expansion of the network to reflect the economic flows.

- Develop railway stations to become hubs for small businesses.

6.4 (b) (ii) Rail privatisation

Medium-Term

- Implement a vertically integrated railway privatisation (especially for freight-based railway).
- Private sector to be encouraged to buy locomotives and operate. Locomotives can be rehabilitated within the $23m estimate made by government
- Identify rail operational assets and maintain them;
- carve out non core assets and use them to settle pensions/other liabilities etc;
- Ensure operators are allowed to operate across the privatised networks via access agreements e.g. at Kaduna junction
- Industry framework – Transport ministry will be restricted to policy and budgeting matters only.

    - a National Railway Development Agency will take ownership of the regulatory setting, and determine public service obligations;

- Rail system shall be all-inclusive – to ensure wide-spread availability of rail services in different parts of the country.

  - Depending on medium term viability, government shall pursue development of new rail infrastructure (rail tracks) via a mix of public and private sector funding;

    - Masterplan to be developed whereby tracks are expanded and the states can plug in to extend services to their hinterland.
    - Lagos-Abuja-Kano as phase I of the masterplan.
    - Phase II to cover other parts of the country.
    - Routes shall be concessioned to private operators post development.

6.5 Specific Initiatives – Lagos

Medium-Term

Undertake operational improvements to significantly decongest Lagos

- Revitalise railways to provide an alternative to trucking of cargoes to and from the port

- Develop a dry port immediately north of Lagos to capture the 70% of containers destined for the Lagos region (the remaining 30% are taken care of under the existing ICD project)
- Such a dry port will provide a container distribution point for cargoes destined for industrial areas north and south of the city

- Develop Onne as a priority project in order to reduce pressure on Lagos, including:

  - completion of the Onne rail link,
  - establishment of the dry port at Aba with a link to the railway, and
  - strengthening the access road from Onne to the A3 Port Harcourt – Enugu road

Enter into a 2G partnership to develop the Lagos mass transit system

- FGN to acquire the land; develop infrastructure and allow operators to run services;
- Lagos to identify and acquire the site; involve private sector in the project as early as possible;
- Identify potential Joint Venture partners for the project and work with them;

- Issue a Lagos rail bond to finance the project
- Grant a concession to a private operator to develop a dedicated power plant (IPP) to service the proposed Lagos rail system

6.6 Funding

Funding estimates for infrastructure improvements and network expansion are in the region of $1 billion per annum for the next 20 years.

SECTION III

LAW & ORDER / CORRUPTION

7.1 The Issues

The deterioration in the country's infrastructure is matched by a similar deterioration in the law and order system. The fact is that Nigeria today is a country in the midst of a social crisis – a crisis reflected in the increasing deterioration in the country's law and order system. The most symbolic manifestation of this situation is the increasing inability of the Nigerian state to protect the lives and properties of its citizens, and to impose its authority over large swathes of armed groups of people across the length and breadth of the country.

Whether Ethnic militia, Area boys, Bakassi boys, Yan daba, Yan kallare etc, sizeable groups have emerged which molest and terrorise innocent people and boldly challenge the state's authority, and with each successful mission, the groups become further emboldened. Where they are caught, the judicial system is not sufficiently configured to efficiently dispense justice while the prisons are in need of reform before they can reform prisoners. A robust enforcement mechanism is needed for the improvement of the investment climate. Investors are deterred by the failure of dispute resolution.

It is therefore ironic that in the aftermath of a return to democracy, the nation's institutions for and system of law and order should continue to deteriorate. It is even more ironic that in a democratic system, governments across all tiers (Federal; State and Local Government) should contribute to this state of affairs by consistently disobeying court orders/rulings thereby encouraging others in disregarding court orders/rulings. All the major institutions (the Police, the Judiciary, the Prisons) are in need of structural transformation, that is., a concerted and well co-ordinated effort is needed to improve access to justice, law enforcement capabilities and the state of Nigerian prisons.

7.2 The Initiatives

Short-Term

Reform of criminal justice system

It is therefore imperative that Nigeria undertakes a comprehensive reform of its criminal justice system. In this regard, the issue of sanctions is paramount. Notwithstanding the fact that they have a significant influence over the peoples behaviour, sanctions have been largely absent in Nigerian public life. Both the Executive Branch and the Legislature must provide examples to the public. The example <u>MUST</u> come from the very top.

- The existing system is largely dysfunctional. The next government shall explicitly make a commitment to **ALWAYS OBEY COURT ORDERS**.
- The Executive shall make it very clear that all agencies/officials shall always respect the rulings of courts etc.
- Government will through words, actions and deeds show that it has a policy of zero tolerance towards official rascality.
- A process of education will be undertaken to ensure that players in the system fully understand their roles;

8. Judiciary

Over the recent years, the corruption that is prevalent in larger society has been allowed to permeate the judiciary, thereby potentially affecting its independence. While it is difficult to provide evidence of this phenomenon, the number of cases brought before the National Judicial Council (NJC) in recent years is symptomatic of this trend. A reform of the system is needed to restore the judiciary's independence. True independence of the judiciary is CRITICAL to the entrenchment of democracy.

To ensure that, the government must respect the sanctity of laws as well as ensure their enforcement.

1ˢᵗ 100 days

- Convene a summit of stakeholders in the administration of justice (police, courts, individuals etc) with the objective of tracing through the problems and recommending fundamental reforms;

Short-Term

- Strengthen the National Judicial Council (NJC) which recommends Judges for appointment;

- Encourage the use of alternative dispute resolution mechanisms side by side with the reform of the administration of justice, in order to decongest the courts and provide a quicker and cost effective mechanism for dispute resolution;

- Ensure financial autonomy for judicial officers both at the official and personal level. This means that conditions of service for Federal Judges should be made comparable to that of Federal legislators; Federal judges must be provided an incentive structure that will make them comfortable for the rest of their lives;

8.1 Federal High Court (FHC)

- Nigeria requires commercial courts for expedited resolution of commercial cases (which presently take a long time to resolve thereby contributing to the systemic risk).

- Commercial courts will improve investor confidence and help to accelerate the administration of justice.

Short-Term

- Expand the scope and refocus the FHC (which has original jurisdiction in matters arising from Federal revenues) to more effectively address commercial cases:

- Sub-divide the FHC into different divisions (admiralty; revenue matters etc); Commercial dispute resolution is critical in attracting investors.
- Introduce a process whereby commercial issues can be resolved within a maximum of 1 year.
- Expand the FHC to become a more effective dispute resolution body.
- Reform FHC rules to allow a fast track process.
- Focus on rapidly building capacity to be able to absorb the number of cases emanating.
- Increase the number of judges in the FHC; There is need to expand the court by attracting a fresh pool of new judges.
- Develop a capacity-building programme side by side with the reform of the FHC (to facilitate specialisation; assist with research etc especially given the opening up of the economy of impending complexity of issues the court will have to rule on e.g., telecoms; power).
- Provide an IT platform that will assist in accelerating the administration of justice and provide easier access to information.

- Adjust the scale of charges at the FHC to encourage alternative dispute resolution processes.

8.2 Federal Court of Appeal

- Reform of the Court of Appeal is also important
- FCA shall be expanded to absorb the number of cases arising

  - Creation of new divisions; and
  - Increasing the capacity of the existing divisions, although without necessarily increasing the access to and costs of taking cases to FCA.

9. Prison System

A holistic reform is required into all aspects/areas of the Nigerian penal system. The following initiatives will be implemented:

1ˢᵗ 100 days

- Convene an all stakeholders summit (including individuals awaiting trial; ex-convicts; prisons staff) that will provide a holistic solution.

Short-Term

- Undertake a fast-track programme to decongest the prisons, especially with respect to awaiting trial cases.

Medium-Term

- **A wholesale improvement in the prisons - the s**tate of prisons is abysmal and will be improved through:

    - improvement in living conditions (health, hygiene; educational facilities)
    - redevelopment of existing prisons
    - Development of new prisons under PPP arrangements

10. The Police

The Nigerian state is increasingly proving incapable of protecting citizens leading to resorting to personalised solutions as exemplified by rise of militia's, private guards, private use of police and the proliferation of small arms. Among the issues that need to be addressed by both government and the citizens include:

1. How to undertake the process of disarming people? That is, a multifaceted approach whereby arms can be given up.
2. The necessity for a nationwide amnesty for the handover of small arms
3. The costs of the reforms and the need to ensure an affordable solution is developed;
4. A change in the concept of policing to bring it nearer to the people (i.e., community based policing). Given the numbers, we must ensure that the **concept of policing is changed**.
5. Improving police officers' morale.
6. Funding for the police
7. Provision of equipment and other logistical support
8. Introduction of a PPP based approach to improve police service delivery.

Harmonisation of local self-protection schemes activities with those of the Police.

10.1 The Initiatives

1ˢᵗ 100 days

- Eliminate the use of police officers under private arrangements i.e., as private security-men and bodyguards;
- Ensure that police officers so released return to mainstream police duties. This will also check the increasing development of a 2-tier police force based on those in mainstream duties and those operating under private arrangements (who have better informal welfare arrangements).
- **Police to provide the Aide de Camps to the President** in a democratic system. There is presently a mind set which favours suppression of the police in favour of the military. The Police must once more be empowered.

Short-Term

- Comprehensive review of the Police conditions of service, including the provision of adequate insurance cover especially given the dangers they face;
- Empowering the Police Service Commission (PSC) and ensuring that appointments of

- senior officers are based on recommendations of the PSC.
- Development of fully functional and equipped forensic laboratories in each of the geo-political zones
- Commence assessment of Commissioners of Police and Divisional Police Officers performances based on crime reduction in their states and divisions.
- Introduction of CCTV networks in key urban hotspots under a collaborative partnership between the Federal and State governments, and the private sector

Medium-Term

- **Strengthen the Police** to enable it undertake its law enforcement responsibilities, and allow the police the latitude to work independently of the Executive arm. Furthermore, action to be taken to enhance police effectiveness and improve the capacity to deter criminal behaviour via:

    i. Better intelligence capabilities/surveillance work
    ii. Training
    iii. Retaining only competent and qualified officers and men
    iv. Provision of adequate firepower
    v. Community based policing

- **Comprehensive review of the Police conditions of service, including the provision of adequate insurance cover especially given the dangers they face;**
- **Introduce concept of Community based policing / Promote localised policing** – i.e., let the states and local communities have a say in the appointment of the Commissioner of Police; Divisional Police Officers etc. under a process that also involves the Police Service Commission

  - Localising does not mean ethnicising the police. There would be limits on the power of the governor to hire and fire.
  - **Police officers presently usually de-linked from Society, They should live within the community** rather than in barracks. Police officers should be encouraged to live within their communities and build their own houses rather than living within barracks etc.
  - Improved collation and publication of divisional crime statistics by division/area

11. Corruption

11.1 The Issues

Notwithstanding the efforts undertaken since 1999 including the creation of new anti-corruption agencies, corruption remains endemic in the Nigerian public and private sectors. Corruption permeates every sphere of Nigerian life, and the **reduction of endemic corruption** within the system must be given priority. The level of corruption is a manifestation of the breakdown of law and order and the absence of an effective enforcement mechanism. There is a perception across the board that rules can be subverted without sanctions. Transparency is a critical starting point for the war against corruption, and values must be reoriented to make the war successful.

The war against corruption **must encompass the police, power, health, educational systems, as well as operate in tandem with the reward and sanctions system**. The systemic problems must be tackled, and people encouraged to inculcate positive values right from very early on via schools and other educational institutions. An explicit **commitment to punish high-level corruption is required, and** people must be brought to book for acts perpetrated). There must be a zero tolerance policy.

11.2 The Initiatives

Short-Term

- Undertake a comprehensive review and increase salaries within the Federal Services, to be financed by improved tax and revenue collection, and reduced leakages:

  - Emphasise the concept of FAIR PAY for FAIR WORK starting with the highest levels of government.
  - Ensure that public workers are adequately rewarded/compensated, thus providing government with the moral authority to sanction errant public workers.
  - Use the wage structure in changing rewards system, with emphasis on merit;

Medium-Term

- Use the educational system as the foundation for the **WAR AGAINST CORRUPTION.**
- Inculcate civics in the basic curriculum of schools and address fundamental corruption related issues from a very early age;

- Social Insecurity (Tackle issues that lead to employee insecurity)
- Accelerated implementation of Pension reforms. Pension reforms will provide the avenue for reduced corruption by creating a long term funding market, and facilitating the development of a consumer credit culture (which will reduce the need for 100% cash outlays for all expenditure), as well as the development of basic infrastructure;
- Facilitate the development of a mortgage market to increase home ownership
- Ensure widespread take off for the National identity card scheme as a mechanism for encouraging development of a credit culture, thereby reducing the need to immediately amass for the sake of affording/acquiring basic consumer items.

12. Civil Service Reform

Reform of the civil service is paramount because an effective and responsive civil service is critical in implementing government's programmes. The mode of operation of the Public sector must change in order for the war against corruption to succeed. Specific initiatives to be pursued are:

Short-Term

- Introduction of a revised civil service rules/procedures that reflect government's increasing service delivery perspective.
- Introduction of Performance Agreements within the public sector – ministries and parastatals shall be required to sign up to clearly defined service delivery targets, and their respective heads will sign performance agreements specifying their deliverables.
- Civil servants shall also be given productivity targets – presently there are no performance indicators or targets, so no basis for holding people responsible.
- Review of civil service compensation packages to bring them in line with market realities.
- Accelerated implementation of the monetisation programme.

- Enhance the quality of the civil service especially supplementing the leadership via infusion of talent from the private sector and the Nigerian diaspora.
- Enforcement of sanctions for errant behaviour.
- Biometrics ascertainment of actual civil service personnel.
- Computerisation of workers records with constant verification.
- Right sizing of work force by providing incentives for workers to leave service early:

  - Those affected shall be empowered via a "fund"/skills acquisition programme to enable them voluntarily exit into a better paying job/occupation.
  - Other incentives include access to agriculture and small business loans.

13. Tax Regime

The tax system will be made an effective partner in the war against corruption. The emphasis of the tax regime shall be on:

- streamlining the tax regime by making it business and investment friendly, and
- enhancing collection of existing taxes

The government will focus on more efficient collection of revenues rather than introduction of new or increases in existing taxes.

Short-Term

- The Federal Inland Revenue Service (FIRS) to be made a mission critical agency for the purpose of not only increasing government revenue but also as an anti-corruption agency. A stronger FIRS is important in:

  - tracking transaction flows within the economy,
  - tracing illicit income and
  - altering behavioural patterns especially in reducing conspicuous consumption associated with illicit earnings

- FIRS to be granted full operational and financial autonomy.
- Implement an initiative to provide for a tax administration system that is robust and which can track payments / plug leakages.
- Inter-agency cooperation and information sharing shall be encouraged between the FIRS, the Economic and Financial Crimes Commission (EFCC) and the Independent Corrupt Practices Commission (ICPC) in order to enhance detection of illicit and or undeclared earnings.
- Introduce a platform for a shared database between FIRS/EFCC/ICPC
- Foster closer working relationships with offshore tax authorities

Medium-Term

- FGN shall facilitate the effective development of an **electronics payment system** nationwide as a means for enhancing tax revenues as well as reducing the velocity of circulation of the Naira.Towards that end, the relevant agencies (FIRS/EFCC/Police/NDLEA) will better utilise the financial sector to monitor transfers/illicit proceeds, and the Central Bank ensuring that local banks implement the financial tracking/monitoring system;

- Strict implementation of tax and money laundering legislation, taking advantage of ongoing international efforts in tackling money laundering

14. Electoral Reforms

Elections are key to democracy. Actors in the political process must be made to respect the law.

14.1 The initiatives

Medium-Term

- Adherence to the law by ensuring appointment of INEC Commissioners and Police Chiefs is made based on recommendations by impartial bodies;
- Process shall be put in place to ensure independence of the Commissioners:

  - INEC funding – should be a first line charge on the consolidated revenue account;
  - INEC should directly submit its budget to the NASS for approval; INEC membership must be of high quality;
  - training required for people who are versed in the electoral process

- Preserve independence of INEC, Police and office of the Attorney-General.
- Provide for a 6-year term for INEC commissioners so that officials oversee the election of a President who did not appoint

of a President who did not appoint them at all times.

- Modified Open Ballot system – counting and announcement of election results immediately after the election.
- Independence of INEC is important BUT is not of itself sufficient to ensure the sanctity of the ballot.
- Independence of Police and Office of the Attorney General of the Federation (AGF) will complement INECs position.
- AGF should be a cabinet level officer who should be recommended to Mr President by the NJC, and who cannot be removed by the Executive (except for gross misconduct etc).
- INEC should provide clear-cut criteria for eligibility for elections. Nothing outside that should be allowed. This will reduce the arbitrary disqualification of candidates.
- Separate office of AGF and Minister of Justice

SECTION IV

THE NIGER DELTA

15.1 The Issues

The state of the Niger Delta remains a scar on the conscience of the Nigerian nation (apologies to Prime Minister Tony Blair). Over the last 50 years, oil has been exploited in commercial quantities and exported, resulting in significant revenues accruing to governments at all levels but with little commensurate development in the oil-producing region to show for it. The Federation and leadership across the board have not been fair to the Niger Delta areas.

The problems afflicting the region are clearly overwhelming, and over time governments at all levels, the leadership and industry operators have proved incapable of providing solutions. The critical issues include:

- Abject poverty in the midst significant revenue generation ability
- Environmental degradation/despoliation issues (gas flaring; degradation; destroyed lives/jobs);
- Low level of economic activity (partly as a result of environmental factors, fishing & farming have been lost as economic activities), manifested in soaring joblessness;
- Limited access to opportunities;

- Feelings of inequitable and unjust treatment by the Nigerian state;
- Clamour for greater share of oil revenues to be retained by the region;
- General state of insecurity manifested by a break down of law and order, the growth of well-armed militias, and the Nigerian state's inability to impose its will and authority. *In some parts of the region, communities have set up their systems of law and order completely independent of the state;*
- Educational drop out rates that are up to three times the rate in the entire south
- In some parts of the region, the incidence of cancers is up to seven times the level in the rest of the country;
- A culture of dependency is in danger of arising unless active efforts are made to address the developmental issues the region faces.

Addressing the Niger Delta issue requires a collaborative effort involving the Federal, State and Local governments (3G partnership). Governments' must come together in order to ensure a region wide solution. Past approaches have unduly emphasised cash transfers at the expense of developmental initiatives that have wide-ranging impact. Solutions shall be developed which go beyond cash, and the Federal

Government must play an active part in these initiatives.

Federal Government direct intervention is required in seriously addressing the problems of the Niger Delta, and The Niger Delta must be treated as a National Emergency Project deserving a "Marshall Plan" to be monitored and supervised at the highest levels of government. Although the FGN will play an active role, the ultimate solutions must be community based with a multi-layered system from ward to local government to state to FGN to focus attention, ensure development and improve the capacity to deliver services.

15.2 The Initiatives

1st 100 days

- Strengthen the Niger Delta Ministry to directly oversee and supervise all Federal Government initiatives in the region.

- Improve and strengthen the amnesty programme beyond the palliatives by prioritizing capacity building and employment generation.

Short-Term

A fundamental change is required –

- Development of a region wide masterplan encompassing the views of all stakeholders
- Consider floating a Niger Delta Bond (to be repaid by pledging proceeds of earnings under a 3G partnership) to significantly increase the quantum of funding immediately needed to undertake development programmes

Medium-Term

- Under a 3G partnership, develop critical infrastructure (township roads; water supply schemes; housing) in urban centres in the region, such as

  - Warri
  - Sapele
  - Ughelli
  - Yenagoa
  - Sagbama
  - Port Harcourt
  - Ikot Abasi

- Education

  - Development of Training and Vocational Centres; vocational centres needed to train people;
  - Introduce stipends for parents to allow their children remain in school;

- Scholarship scheme (in conjunction with oil companies) for students both under- and post graduate studies.

- Security

  - Negotiate with local stakeholders to secure rights over certain routes (pipelines etc).
  - Creation of a Coast Guard under the Naval High Command specially trained for the environment that can patrol the creeks (possibly majority Niger Delta manned) and securing pipelines / tackle illegal bunkering.
  - Involve the oil companies and local leadership in resolving the militia problems prevalent in the area.

- Environmental initiatives

  - Ensure strict enforcement of penalties for gas flaring
  - Accelerated implementation of the gas fiscal regime to encourage greater gas utilisation
  - Major environmental clean-up to be used as a basis for job creation; giving people a sense of belonging

- Social Services

- Create a lower level of health care (community based healthcare care on a lower level than the primary care system and which is preventive)
- Health and education systems to be developed based on settlement patterns (including health and education)
- Deliver brand new systems for delivering social services in the Niger Delta starting from the ground up
- Introduce with active private sector support, an active youth development programme encompassing sports, vocational activity, leisure and recreation that could provide income earning and social mobility potential.

- Develop a framework to expand power beyond existing community leaders because a broader mind set which is required to achieve development.
- Develop the petrochemical industries and other ancillary activities

SECTION V

EDUCATION & SOCIAL SERVICES

16.1 The Issues

Nigerians presently spend in excess of $1 billion annually to acquire education outside the country. At least half that amount is also expended on medical care abroad. This represents a significant leakage in the economy particularly when a fraction of the amount over 5 years can make a huge improvement in the country's health care and educational systems. In 2004, FGN budgeted, N893bn (11% of the budget) for education (excluding UBE and ETF), compared to 21% in Botswana; 26% in Ghana; 22% in Namibia. Nigeria allocates almost 60% of the education budget to tertiary education; 80% of which is recurrent.

The population has doubled in the last 20 years; 50% of the population is under 25 years old; 70% under 40 years. Furthermore, there are 11million primary school pupils yearly, with a drop out rate over 50%; by the secondary school stage, only 4 million places available. About 7 million are therefore lost from the system. At the tertiary level, there are 110,000 university graduates annually and about 140,000 in other tertiary institutions. This means that approximately 3.75 million secondary students cannot be fit into the system –

about 1 million sit for JAMB annually so barely 10% of university applicants end up being admitted.

FUNDING

"No child left behind" policy

The State must pursue a no child left behind policy. The state has a duty (due to the intrinsic value; benefits to society etc) to provide basic education to individuals up to the age of 16. The market is already working for the middle-income groups in terms of obtaining private education.

Market mechanisms should provide the signals for graduates BUT the state has a role to actively promote education in priority sectors so that capacity is developed for graduates that will be required in the future

In addition, the state must create the opportunities for graduates (locally or foreign) to take up positions within the country through schemes such as a diaspora fund (from funding pooled from government and corporate sponsors) whereby specialist positions in government can be filled by people in the diaspora, with the fund ensuring they do not suffer unduly from the lower salaries applicable in the Nigerian public sector.

The State must also pursue policies to provide the absorptive capacity to take graduating students – a National Manpower development plan is thus needed to ascertain the sector's requirements going forward.

The issues surrounding both education and health are the quality, access; staff working conditions and funding.

16.2 The Initiatives

16.2 (i) Education

Short-term

The Government shall introduce a "No child left behind" policy – all schoolchildren upto the age of 16 will be fully taken account of by the government.

- Basic literacy skills are a public good and will be supported by the state

  - therefore education up to 16 years of age shall be publicly funded;
  - Beyond the minimum required, people should buy from the private sector etc but government should provide the opportunity for education

- Scholarships will be provided for a defined number of students at the tertiary level;

- Quality standards shall be introduced for artisans (City & Guilds type certification) to be able to absorb/train a minimum of 100,000 artisans annually;
- Introduction of verifiable indicators of the UBE performance
- Manage transition/crisis in the education system –change in the 6-3-3-4 system has potential to confuse. An effective transition plan must be in place.
- Change the Federal Government's role in education:

  - to function as a regulator

    - set certifications of quality;
    - define standards for vocational; technical; other education
    - Monitor compliance with the standards

  - Awarding scholarships to bright but indigent students in each geo-political zone.
  - Develop special programmes for exceptionally gifted students in all the geo-political zones.
  - Encourage the state governments, businesses and wealthy individuals to award scholarships to bright and indigent students.

- Encourage continuing vocational education for those who have left schools.

Medium-Term

- Under the 3G partnership, develop a framework to enable the following have responsibility for education at the various levels

  - Primary – Local governments and the private sector
  - Secondary – State governments and the private sector
  - Post secondary – State governments and the private sector
  - to enable it function as a regulator

- FGN shall own 1 university in each geo-political zones

  - Develop them as centres of excellence
  - The universities shall be encouraged to charge user fees at market rates under the 3G partnership, develop a framework to enable the following have responsibility for education at the various levels
  - Return remaining universities to the states or place them under trustees

- Commit to a certain % of the budget to education – this will be done under a collaborative process and within the 3G partnership
- Introduce realistic fees in the university system; free up funding which would be devoted to primary and secondary education
- Empower people to take charge of their own lives
- Use NYSC camps for training 10 months out of every year. Set up mobile training centres with a level of certification/standardisation; some graduates could go on to university.
- Quality: - Teacher training – Emergency programme to be developed to enhance standards as well as achieve improved remuneration to encourage teachers to remain in the sector.
- FGN to return some universities to the states – maintain one in each geo-political zone.

16.2 (ii) Health

Nigeria has the worst human development index (HDI) statistics in Africa (among non-war ravaged countries). The 4 major ailments/killers are:

- HIV
- Malaria
- Maternal mortality
- Infant mortality

The government's efforts would therefore be concentrated on these four ailments as well as providing primary and community based health care.

The general initiatives are presented below:

1ˢᵗ *100 days*

- Health related matters shall reside within the Federal Ministry of Health. Based on a concerted anti-corruption campaign, up to $1bn in leakages can be captured and a significant amount channelled into health related issues. Savings made can be across the board.

Medium-Term

- Change the emphasis of health programmes so that the basic preventive solutions start from the base – from the local communities.

  - FGN to be in charge of health at the top and shall drive the process with the states/LGs actually responsible for implementation.
  - FGN's role will be to lay down policy guidelines, fund research in collaboration with the states, coordinate the efforts –

- FGN emphasis shall be on the tertiary (teaching hospitals, assisted procurement programmes);
- Funding shall be joint with states/LGs.
- FGN will provide policy guidance framework as opposed to active participation

16.2 (ii) (a) HIV-Aids

Nigeria has a 5% HIV prevalence rate; the 3rd highest incidence worldwide. Only 100,000 are reached via Anti Retro Viral treatments (ARVs). Generally, we have not reacted well enough to the HIV scourge. Amongst others, government will over the short term do the following:

1. Ensure widespread access to ARVs.
2. Provide adequate preventive health care amongst the young (where HIV is spreading fastest) - In addition, HIV is not only an urban problem – some of the highest incidences have been in largely rural populations in the Middle Belt.
3. Provide accessible voluntary counselling and testing (VCT) centres. These need to be introduced, and will help in tackling the spread of HIV-AIDS. Uganda and Kenya have been successful using this approach.

4. Support additional sensitisation and education especially via community-based programmes.

16.2 (ii) (b) Malaria

Malaria is the biggest health problem in the country; Nigeria has capacity to supply its entire chloroquine needs but needs to find a way to solve the fake/incomplete drugs issue; In some areas, incidences of fake chloroquine is almost 100%.

The following specific programmes shall be implemented:

- Encourage pharmaceutical companies to locally provide chloroquine which is now non-patented.
- Provide a sustained nationwide **environmental response** (sprays; introduction of sanitary inspectors etc as a sustainable programme to complement the **bednet system which has had limited effectiveness**
- Cross-border cooperation - Concerted efforts to be made with our neighbours in order to ensure that our environmental response is complemented by similar efforts across our borders.
- Major health problems that are environmental are always heavier in the coastal areas. There will be a concerted effort at

preventive strategies (stagnant water – cholera linkage, reaching out to countries where malaria has been reduced)

16.2 (ii) (c) Maternal Mortality

Childbirth is a high-risk enterprise in Nigeria (unlike in other countries); Nigeria loses 30/1000 mothers at childbirth. Only a third of childbirth is in a controlled environment (i.e., an environment where you can make a response and record/register the birth of a child/death of the mother etc).

The short-term initiatives to be implemented include:

- Provision of info (literature; helplines etc) which assuage peoples concerns; to provide enough info and solutions to the poor to enable kids have a chance of survival.
- Sensitisation and increased awareness of simple solutions such as oral rehydration therapy (ORT)
- Introducing the concept of localising the problems by community nursing/midwives, and providing community health workers;
- Federally assisted training programme for health workers in urban and rural areas

16.2 (ii) (d) Infant mortality

1 in 5 of all Nigerian children are lost by the age of 5 years – the cause of death is primarily malaria related. The solutions required are similar to those that will be implemented for maternal mortality.

Atiku Abubakar Policy Group